Antarctica

By Allan Fowler

Consultant
Linda Cornwell
Coordinator of School Quality and Professional Improvement
Indiana State Teachers Association

Children's Press®
A Division of Grolier Publishing
New York London Hong Kong Sydney
Danbury, Connecticut

Visit Children's Press® on the Internet at:
http://publishing.grolier.com

Designer: Herman Adler Design Group
Photo Researcher: Caroline Anderson
The photo on the cover shows a portion of Antarctica's icy landscape.

Library of Congress Cataloging-in-Publication Data

Fowler, Allan.
    Antarctica / by Allan Fowler.
      p. cm. — (Rookie read-about geography)
    Includes index.
    Summary: An introduction to the continent of Antarctica, its
geographical features, visitors, and animals.
    ISBN 0-516-21669-4 (lib. bdg.)   0-516-27297-7 (pbk.)
    1. Antarctica—Juvenile literature. [1. Antarctica.] I. Title. II. Series.
G863.F68   2001
919.8'9—dc21

                                 00-027561

GROLIER
PUBLISHING

The biggest pieces of land on Earth are called continents.

There are seven continents.

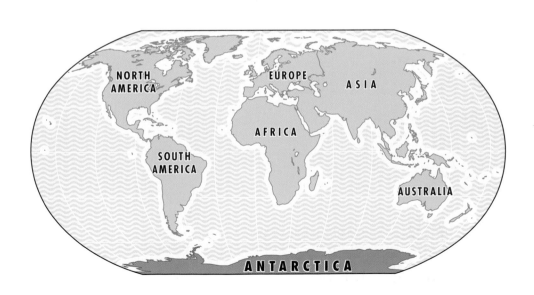

Antarctica (ant-AR-tik-uh)
is the coldest continent.
Ice and snow cover most
of the land.

You can find Antarctica
on a globe of the Earth.

The North Pole is shown
at the top of the globe.

The South Pole is shown at
the bottom, in Antarctica.

Frozen rivers of ice, called glaciers (GLAY-shurs), move slowly across Antarctica.

Cliffs of ice rise high
above the coasts, or
edges, of the continent.

Scientists at work in Antarctica

No one lives in Antarctica, but some people visit.

Most of the visitors are scientists. They study the continent's water, land, and weather.

During the summer, the sun stays out almost all day in Antarctica.

It does not get very dark outside at night.

A summer night in Antarctica

14

Antarctica is always cold. Even in the summer, tall mountains are covered with snow.

In the winter, the sun hardly comes out at all. Afternoons can be as dark as nights.

A winter day in Antarctica

During the winter, more
ice forms around the coasts
of the continent.

Big chunks of the ice
break off into the ocean
and float away.

These pieces of floating
ice are called icebergs.

22

There are no trees in Antarctica. Only the simplest plants, such as moss, grow there.

Only a few animals live in Antarctica. In the summer, big groups of penguins (PEN-gwins) crowd the coasts.

Whales swim in the ocean.

Some other types of birds and tiny insects also live in Antarctica.

Even though Antarctica is a lonely continent, there are many amazing things to see and study there.

Words You Know

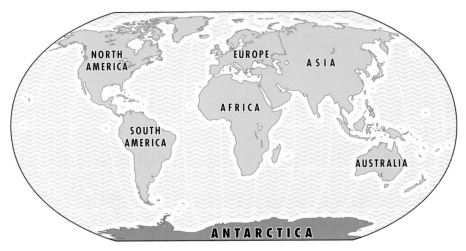

continents

glaciers

globe

30

icebergs

moss

penguins

scientists

31

Index

About the Author

Allan Fowler is a freelance writer with a background in advertising. Born in New York, he now lives in Chicago and enjoys traveling.

Photo Credits

Photographs ©: Nance S. Trueworthy: 7, 30 right; Peter Arnold Inc.: 22, 31 top right (Fred Bruemmer), 24, 31 bottom left (Fritz Polking), 13 (Galen Rowell), 27 (Roland Seitre), 17 (Gordon Wiltsie); Photo Researchers: 4 (Bill Bachmann), 25 (Tim Davis), 9, 10, 21, 31 top left, 31 bottom right (Joyce Photographics), 8, 14, 30 left (George D. Lepp), 18 (Rod Planck); Tony Stone Images: 28 (Tim Davis), cover (Johnny Johnson).

Map by Bob Italiano.